Looking Back at Lynn

A Scrapbook of the 50s & 60s

Tricky Sam Publishing

Foreword

Why did everything seem so much better in the 50s? A lot of us didn't have TV, inside lavatories, central heating, washing machines – some of us had no bathroom. There was no running hot water – the trusty kettle that made the tea also provided the hot water for the bath. The floors were either bare board or lino – wall to wall carpet was unheard of.

But we didn't live in a crime-ridden society where ill discipline, bad manners, selfishness, un-friendliness, greed and violence were commonplace.

People were neighbourly, there was a job for life, children were safer – and could roam and explore the town and countryside safely. Now the volume of traffic has driven them off the streets. As a twelve year old, in the school holidays, I was allowed to buy a weekly railway rover ticket and go off on my own to places like Peterborough or Norwich and spend all day sitting on station platforms train spotting, only returning in time for tea - and public transport ran on time.

You didn't need modern electronic gadgets because you learnt to think for yourself. You could add up in your head, could make reasoned decisions and you were resourceful. Your reward was the satisfaction of achievement whether it was making a model, swimming ten lengths at the baths or working for a few bob after school delivering groceries for one of the many grocers in town. If you were in full time employment, doing a good day's work (job satisfaction), you were valued by your boss. You certainly were never bored because you used your brain and did not have to rely on TV, computer games or someone else to entertain you.

Perhaps life today has become too easy and there is no incentive – that sense of achievement has been lost and as human beings that was always our raison d'etre.

People no longer feel at home in their communities. The fifties was a gentler era when manners and people mattered. People were more important than possessions and they had time for each other, knew their neighbours and had a sense of belonging.

The start of the sixties was a continuation of the 50s but the second half were the years of change – possibly the start of the steady decline!

The catch phrase at the beginning of the sixties 'you've never it had so good' seemed to spark the drive towards a selfish society and consumerism, but those who lived through these earlier years still have affectionate memories of that gentler time.

Acknowledgements

My sincere thanks to all the following who have loaned me photographs and helped with information relating to many of the photographs.

Dick Goodchild	Winifred Chilvers	Ian Smith
Lynn News	Bob Hall	David Fleming
Jim Tuck	Peter Mott	Norfolk County Council
David Andrews	Marion Hornigold	All the staff at Central Library, King's Lynn
Eddie Lyon	Ann Kerry	Colin Bailey (Dawbarns Pearson)
Peter Todhunter	Colin King	Rick Meek
Colin Fysh	Reg Knight	Eastern Daily Press
Roger Carter	Chris Holt	John Allen
John Bunting	Michael Booth	Carol Dilks
Sheila Broughton	Tony Skerritt	Neville Everett
Dennis Walker	John King	Neville Brown
Ray Bullock	Gary Madge	Robert Fuller
David Leveritt	Tony Jubey	Brian Fisher
June Walker	Peter Earl	Vivienne Marler

Thanks to John and Sarah for proof reading and to Janet for her help with the cover design.

Introduction

Every effort has been made to trace the originators of all of the photographs if not already known.
A very small number of photos have appeared in other publications but I felt their inclusion here was necessary for the continuity of the book. In some cases, where the date of the photograph is uncertain, a 'best estimate' or anecdotal evidence has been used.
Many descriptions relating to some photos are derived from 'word of mouth' and therefore, may not be precise through the mists of time.
Owing to the diversity of the sources of the photos the quality of some are not as good as I would have preferred but, if the photo is of real interest, I think the sacrifice is worth its inclusion.
I have tried to maintain a chronological theme through the book (starting 1950) and, at the same time, keep related photos together - unfortunately this was not always possible, thus the flow may appear a bit disjointed. That said, I think the photographic interest more than compensates.

The copyright use of photographs from the Lynn News, West Norfolk Borough Council and the Eastern Daily Press is acknowledged and gratefully appreciated.

For Janet, Sarah and John

Copyright © Bob Booth 2007

First Printed 2007
Revised and reprinted 2011

Published by Tricky Sam Publishing

Email: trickysampublishing@tiscali.co.uk

Printed by Clanpress, King's Lynn

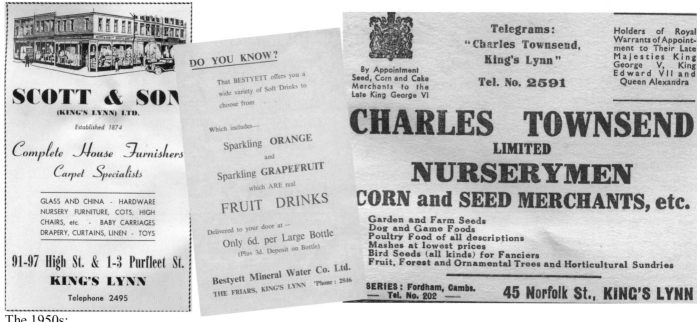
The 1950s:

In 1950 the Eagle comic (remember Dan Dare) was launched. Tide washing powder first reached the shops. The restrictions on petrol, paper and soap were ended. We listened to Dick Barton on the wireless. Long Playing records (33⅓ rpm) first appeared.

There were very few families with a television (700,000 viewers) as the cost relative to the average wage was beyond most. Also there was only one transmitter at Alexandra Palace and the signal strength was very weak - to receive any sort of picture you needed a 50ft. aerial mast and live at Brow of the Hill, Leziate!

In 1951 there was the Festival of Britain and, for many of us schoolboys, it was our first school trip and, more than likely, our first trip to London. In 1952 the King died at Sandringham. Sooty and the Flowerpot Men first appeared the TV screen.

1953 saw the floods (31st January). Sweet rationing ended in February. The coronation of the Queen followed. 100,000 televisions were sold in this year because of the coronation. The screen size was 12inches (14 for the wealthy) black & white of course! The Morris Oxford first appeared on the roads.

1954 saw Stork margarine, Maxwell House coffee, Wagon Wheels and tea bags along with Omo all reach the grocers shelves. This was also the watershed year when Rock 'n' Roll made a major impact—who can forget Bill Haley's 'Rock Around the Clock'? By 1955 only 30% of homes had a refrigerator. Birdseye fish fingers were introduced. 45 rpm single records were starting to challenge the 78 rpm, easily breakable, shellac records. In this year filter tip cigarettes only accounted for 2% of the market—most popular brands were Players Navy Cut and Senior Service.

1956 The Lone Ranger was first seen on TV and in May we first heard Elvis Presley (Heartbreak Hotel). At one of our three cinemas we could go to see High Society and Hollywood or Bust (Dean Martin & Jerry Lewis). Corgi models appeared in toy shops as a rival to Dinky toys.

1957 There were now 7 million viewers watching TV when Dixon of Dock Green made his debut. Rothmans King size cigarettes went on sale. Premium bonds were introduced.

1958 Introduction of Flash, Handy Andy & Camay soap (with that annoying TV advert 'You'll be a little lovelier each day…'). Stereo records.

1959 The Mini arrived—I remember Peter Guests on Wootton Road had one of the first for sale—I was offered it when I went to buy my first new vehicle (an Austin A35 van) but turned it down - it was too small to ever catch on!

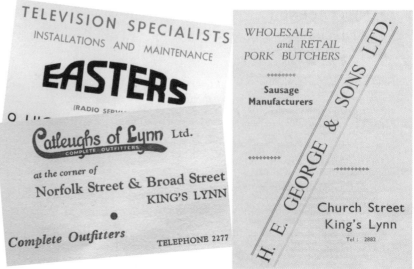

ABOVE:
Beaulah's in 1950. Beaulah's Canners Ltd. was opened in 1932 adjacent to F Savage's engineering works in Estuary Road. By the late 1960s it had become Anglia Canners. There appear to be at least four supervisors keeping 'an eye' on the workforce.

BELOW:
The 1950 St Georges Day scout parade is in progress at St Faith's church, Gaywood. Leading the procession is the scout master of the 14th Wootton troop, Charlie Bew, a very popular and respected man in the scouting movement. Behind him is his troop, followed by the 15th and 12th Gaywood troops.

RIGHT:
The staff of
Catleughs' of Lynn,
outfitters. This picture and
the two interior pictures of
this large firm were taken
about 1950.
They had a virtual
monopoly on the sale of
school uniforms and the
picture (mid-right) is of the
boys and girls department.
Mr Catleugh was an
alderman and prominent
figure in the town, having
been a leading figure in the
slum clearance of the
1930s. He passionately
believed in providing
better homes for the town's
residents.

RIGHT:
This picture, taken in
1950, shows the
difference in the size
of businesses in the
town.
The Watch Shop was
owned and run by
Mr & Mrs W Rees.
The shop was on the
corner of St James
Street and Church
Street next to
Pratt & Coldham,
hairdressers.
It was demolished in
the mid 60s.
The owners pose in
the shop doorway.

TOP RIGHT:
November 1950 looking south up Tower Street. The man is standing at the entrance to South Clough Lane. Bayes at 6, Tower Street was a wireless business started by Charlie Bayes in 1928 at 7, Tower Street - across the road from No.6. After the war two entrepreneurs bought the business, which my father managed until he subsequently became owner in the late 50s. Besides selling radios, the odd TV and electrical goods the shop's other main function was to charge accumulator batteries for country customers who did not have an electricity supply.

7, Tower Street at this time belong to Jimmy & Jean Dawson who ran it as the Book & Toy Shop. Everyone in the street knew Jimmy who was a very knowledgeable man, particularly on the workings of the town's electricity system. Some parts of the town still ran on DC and Jimmy was one of a very few who understood the vagaries of the town circuits.

The shop next to Bayes (No. 8) is currently empty. In 1954 was to open as the Pink Grill café.

MIDDLE RIGHT:
A sunny November (1950) late morning with a view up Tower Street.

RIGHT:
December 1950.
It is Christmas at the hospital - at this time on Hospital Walk, off London Road.
Sisters, besides all their other duties, find time to organise a candle-lit procession through the wards singing carols for the benefit of the patients.

The hospital closed in 1982 when the new Queen Elizabeth Hospital opened on Gayton Road.

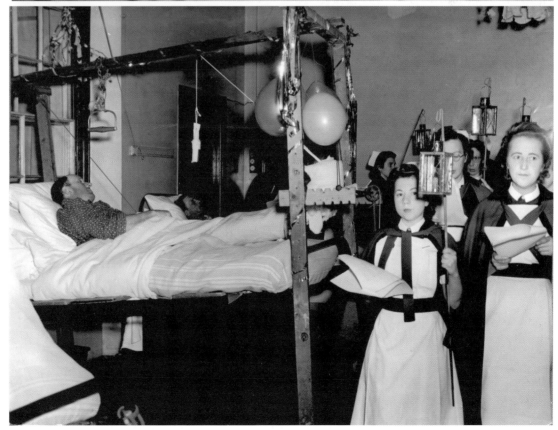

As seen in the Lynn News

Incorporating LYNN ADVERTISER (Est. 1841), LYNN NEWS (Est. 1860), Etc.

10,601   Tel. 2692/2693   TUESDAY, NOVEMBER 27, 1951.   Postage 1½d.   Price 3d.   MURDIN 19, ST. JAMES' S

IN MINIATURE   Nearly 13,000 roared delight at this

IMMEDIATELY after this picture was taken the 12,931 crowd at Lynn Walks gave their mightiest roar of the day. It marked the scoring | of Lynn's equalising goal after 25 minutes of Saturday's cup-tie against Exeter. Scorer Cliff Whitelum can be seen on the ground just | in front of goalkeeper Lear who had made an unsuccessful attempt to intercept a right wing cross. Also behind Whitelum is Lynn | winger Morris. Centre-forward Everitt watches the ball enter the net as right back Warren turns in a desperate attempt to reach | the ball. Whitelum was mobbed by his colleagues and it was seconds before he could rise from the ground. Below: IS EVERYBODY | HAPPY? It would certainly seem so from this picture of part of the crowd in jubilant mood.

BELOW: A welder hurries to complete the installation of new retorts which will overcome the gas shortage in town. Gas pressures throughout the town had to be reduced because the old plant could not produce enough gas to meet demand.
The works was first built in 1825 to supply gas light to replace whale oil lamps & tallow candles.
At the gasworks, the gas was generated by distilling coal. The process, now superseded by the supply of natural gas, also produced coke and coal tar from which a host of chemicals were made.
The works was dismantled in the mid 60s.

ABOVE:
In November 1951 King's Lynn played Exeter in a cup tie.
BELOW:
August 1951 - the war had only been over six years and people were just starting find out how to enjoy themselves again. Forget going abroad - Hunstanton and Heacham were the places where many of us had great holidays!

No. 10,569   Tel. 2692/2693   TUESDAY, AUGUST 7, 1951.

10,000 RAIL TRIPPERS IN DAY AT HUNS'TON
Record for B.R., —not for traders

AFTER THE BUSIEST WEEK since the war Hunstanton sea front traders and cafe proprietors were confidently looking forward to a record week-end but the weather faltered.

After a dull cloudy and wet day on Saturday they were were still hopeful but less confident. Sunday provided them with a bumper day, but yesterday morning's early showers and grey skies had their effect on day trippers.

HOWEVER, THE HOLIDAY DID PRODUCE SOME POST-WAR RECORDS IN THE NUMBER OF VISITORS ARRIVING AT THE COAST BY RAIL, HUNSTANTON STATION ALONE HANDLING OVER 10,000 PEOPLE.

A number of people in Hunstanton for the day on Saturday disregarded the ominous-looking clouds and took deck-chairs on to the beach early in the afternoon, but soon they were rushing for shelter as the first spots of rain began to fall.

For the rest of the day rain fell intermittently, the beach was deserted, and trade on the sea front practically at a standstill.

Sunday fell between two stools. Despite the fine

At Wells

Throughout the week preceding the holiday there was a steady stream of visitors at Wells absorbing all the available accommodation. The number of resident visitors at the week-end was easily a record. All hotels and boarding houses were full, and many late comers were unfortunate.

Train traffic during the week was the heaviest for several years. Two Sunday morning trains took over 2,000

HUNST'ON'S BUSIEST WEEK

NOT for many years has Hunstanton had such a busy week as last week. Trippers poured into the town in their thousands by train, coach, car and bicycle, and the sea front traders and cafe proprietors were nearly run off their feet.

Said one cafe proprietor: "It has been our busiest week ever. In fact if there had been thousands more people in we could not have done more business. There are not

RIGHT: 1951 Queen Mary Road. Forget computer games & the rest, we could amuse ourselves playing fives. Left to right: John Petts, Jean Fulcher, June Fulcher, Sonny Wiffen, Doreen Johnson, Sheila Fulcher & Pamela Fulcher are watched by an audience.

On parade

ABOVE:
The King's Lynn Players put on 'Hit The Deck' at the Pilot February & March 1951. Produced by Fred Calvert (in check shirt) and Dorothy McDonald (in front of piano) was the musical director. Eddie Lyon who has been a prolific producer of later shows is fourth from the right.

LEFT:
The annual cadet inspection by Colonel Boag at the Grammar School in 1951. It was reported that:
'*During the afternoon demonstrations were put on by the company. The colonel did criticise the handling of the rifles*'.
Thursday afternoons were set aside for cadet training. Though not compulsory, anyone not joining was looked upon unfavourably - but at least some of us got our homework done early to leave the evening free!

RIGHT:
24th July 1951.
The Queen inspects troops in King Street.

The King's Lynn Festival had been inaugurated in 1950, here The Queen was attending the second festival.

TOP: 1951. Gaywood Park cricket teams.
ABOVE: Summer 1951.
At King's Lynn Corporation Swimming Pool (or better known as 'The Baths') are the girls of Gaywood Park's Marlborough House, winners of the inter-house swimming competition.

TOP RIGHT:
All Saint's Hall in 1951.
Miss Bligh's Music School.
Included here are: Michael Woods,
Roland Metcalf, David Andrews, Barry
Ballard, Michael Plume, Peter Bensley,
Prunella Bensley, Ray Snushall, Mike
Bloom, possibly three Simper
brothers and, in the centre sitting is,
Miss Bligh.

RIGHT: 1951 Lower Canada, outside the
Engineers Tavern, corner of Blackfriars Road &
Coburg St.
A group of friends pose for the camera.
They include Ray Anderson, David Anderson,
Peter Earl, Wilf Ellis, Violet Howard, Derek Earl,
Janice Lusher, Terry Gill, David Loasby (whose
parents kept the pub) and Dusty the dog.

BELOW:
December 1952.
The Grammar School put on a production of the
operetta The Batsman's Bride.
At this time any collaboration with the High
School was not on.
The onerous job of dressing in women's clothes
was forced on the first year boys since they were
the only boys in the school who could sing falsetto
notes as their voices hadn't broken.

TOP:
1952. The girls of The Convent rehearse The Mikado in the school hall. The correct name for the school was 'The Servite Convent' and was situated at 39 & 41 Goodwins Road.
The senior school closed in 1969 and the following year the junior school closed.

ABOVE:
In 1952 Gaywood Park staged a music festival. Here the conductor (Mr F Bone) works his way through a rehearsal.

ABOVE: Top yard, King's Lynn. In November 1952 a shunting engine, in its hurry to get down the yard, jumped the points. There were around 150 of these engines (built between 1890 & 1904), originally used as passenger engines for working the London suburban trains. As the trains got heavier they were relegated to be used as shunting engines and could be found in most Eastern Anglian railway yards. They had earned the nickname of 'buckjumpers'!

RIGHT:
South Lynn.
In August 1952 this depot also had a mishap when the locomotive, not fully in steam, was pushed on to the turntable by another locomotive. As it was being turned, somehow it suddenly 'found' enough steam to move forward when halfway round.
It took 11 hours to jack it up and re-rail it.

RIGHT:
High Street in 1952. A company representative (or travellers as they were then called) carries his samples down towards Jermyn's. Bowler hats seemed to be the order of the day for office workers and travellers! Meanwhile, a well-dressed lady comes out of Le Grice with her purchases. Hunters Tea Stores is on the corner of Baker Lane. Next door is Jane Hole's children's outfitters.

LEFT:
High Street 1952.
The morning sun has now broken through. Three young women have just come out of Jermyn's. On the left is Salter & Salter (footwear), Adcock's (tobacconists), Fifty Shilling Tailors, Hollywood Hats and Winton-Smith (ham & beef dealers).

For a full list of High Street shops refer to pages 47 & 48.

RIGHT:
Broad Street in 1952. Note the cobbled street.
The Grosvenor Restaurant.
The address was actually 13, Norfolk Street. It was owned at the time by Alec Goodwin, a well known local entrepreneur.
Kelly's Street Directory describes it as: *'fully licensed restaurant & snack bar, parties catered for'*. It had opened in 1769 and finally closed in 1969, when it was swept away by the (then) new development.
The man on the right is window shopping at Catleugh's.

There is a sale on at HJ Wilson Ltd. (costumiers) in Norfolk Street.

TOP: The Millfleet, 1953.

A general view of the 'fleet', as it was commonly known. The Library is at the top of the fleet on the left.

There were about 1000 departures a week from here, operated by 140 bus services.

The main operators were the Eastern Counties & the Lincolnshire Roadcar Co. along with dozens of private operators who only ran services into the fleet on Tuesdays and Saturdays.

ABOVE: Shows the fleet in 1955.

The Hunstanton bus (service 35) departs from the bus-stop in front of the Morris Minor. A girl waves to a friend on the departing bus. The bus-stop beyond that was the departure point for the South Wootton (service 39), Gaywood Park (service 39A) and Newlyn (service 39B) buses. The building on the left was the rather notorious toilets!

ABOVE:
By 1953 the Grammar School had expanded when its normal intake of 60 pupils increased to 90, thus creating three streams in the first year. Two new houses were created (Gloucester & Edinburgh). The six existing houses were Windsor, Keene, Lancaster, Thoresby, School and York.

Here the newly formed Gloucester House pose for the camera.

RIGHT: 1953 was the Coronation of The Queen. Here a group of children dress up for the occasion in Estuary Close

Not one car in sight along here - only bicycles!

The low late morning sun casts a shadow across St James Street in early 1953.
The Three Pigeons pub is open for business. The pub closed in 1957 when it became Green & Wright, Ltd, wine & spirit merchants & beer retailers. This street was called Three Pigeons Street before it got its current name.

As seen in the Lynn News

Worthy addition to architecture of ancient town

LEFT:
In 1953 Lynn's new Police station was nearing completion when the Lynn News published this picture. The report stated that '*the sweeping façade is an adornment to the town, a worthy piece of modern architecture to take its place in a town rich with ancient beauty*'.
It's hard to imagine any miscreant seeing it quite like that on being arrested!
It was stated that the building would be completed by the end of the year.

RIGHT:
In 1953 The Lynn News reported that *'Littleport Street is Lynn's "Black Spot" so far as accidents are concerned'*.
The inset photo was part of a large-scale map of the town which Police kept to maintain a record of the number of accidents which had taken place so far in this year.
Each pin signified an accident and there were more here than anywhere else in town.
The photographer is standing near Kettlewell Lane, looking towards the town centre.

Lynn's 'Black spot' for road accidents

RIGHT:
In 1953 willing helpers get stuck in decorating and cleaning up the old Methodist Church School Hall in Tower Street .
The Youth Centre was a great place to meet, with a wide range of activities from table tennis to quiz nights.

There was a main hall and one or two smaller rooms for fringe activities. One of which was a record session of swing music (Ted Heath, Benny Goodman) which, along with one or two of us Grammar School boys, was mainly attended by Teddy Boys - united in music!

Their part in giving Lynn a youth centre

WHERE there's a will there's a way. That is the motto of members of the Thursday Youth Club, who don their oldest clothes each Tuesday and Thursday evening to clean up and redecorate the Tower Street Methodist Hall, Lynn, in its conversion into a new youth centre for the town. Some club members are pictured here at work last Thursday evening.

TOP:
A class photo from Gaywood Park School in 1953, which had opened in September 1939.
I believe the opening had to be postponed by one week owing to the declaration of the war.

ABOVE:
In 1954 the town celebrated the 750th anniversary of the granting of Lynn's first charter (14th September 1204). The procession passes the South Gate. Leading the parade are Bobby Holman (left) and Eddie Lyon (right). The parade had started on the Tuesday Market and eventually finished on the Walks where 10 episodes representing the 750 years were enacted.

ABOVE:
Across the road from the Youth Centre in Tower Street was another popular place to meet - the Roller Skating Rink.

The building was originally a Wesleyan Methodist Chapel that had first opened in 1813.

In 1954 the skaters pose in their fancy dress outfits.

The building was eventually demolished in 1960 when the site was purchased by William King, the Ford car dealer.

I think the floor was asbestos - health & safety!!

RIGHT:
Swimmers at the King's Lynn Corporation Public Swimming Bath (or The Baths) in The Walks pose on the fountain in summer 1954.

In the summer months (there was no heating) this was very popular and, sometimes in the school holidays, you were rationed to one hour in the pool. This was done by completely clearing the pool before the next group (queuing outside) were allowed in.

Most children bought a season ticket (10 shillings). The temperature of the pool usually ranged (depending on the weather) from about 48°F to 68°F.

The Baths had opened in 1921 and closed in 1975. It was left derelict until 1980 when it was filled in.

BELOW:
This photo, taken at the Baths in 1954, is in fact the Baths Water Polo team with their Teddy Boy outfits on. The sign reads 'Teddy Boys V Old Codgers' - as they had just played a match against a team of (slightly) older members of the club.

They are from left to right: David Bucke, David Leveritt, David Howard, Joe Terry, Norman Hastings, Douglas Simpson and Derek Warnes.

ABOVE:
Two more pictures taken in the Skating Rink in 1954. Skaters pose for the camera as they display their skating competition numbers.

BOTTOM RIGHT:
An American serviceman is given a 'spin' by one of the more accomplished skaters.

BOTTOM LEFT:
Another view of the Baths probably taken about the same time as the picture on the previous page.
The swimmers are in the shallow end (4ft) - I believe the deep end was 6ft 6ins - but not being a very good swimmer, I did not venture down that end too often.

TOP LEFT:

This TV & general domestic electrical shop was at 58/59 Norfolk Street. The shop was built in 1953 by my father & uncle but it had to be built some 20ft back because it was intended to widen this part of Norfolk Street. The street, at this time, was the main route into town from the east and north. This put the business at a disadvantage (being partially obscured by its neighbours) and it only lasted a very short time. Recently the site has been cleared.

TOP RIGHT:

Looking east down Norfolk Street towards Townsend's Corner in 1954. Next to ER Giles (electrical engineers) is Paradise Lane leading to the cattle market.

MIDDLE RIGHT:

St Nicholas Street in 1959. The buildings on the right of the picture were replaced by the Employment Exchange. The corner leading to the Tuesday Market is still a bottle neck.

RIGHT:

This picture was taken in 1955. Chilvers opened in 1914 and was on the corner of Littleport Street and Austin Street. Although there was a garage it specialised in sales of new cycles & accessories. Cycle repairs were carried out in the garage part by one man, Arthur Chambers, who could mend anything relating to bikes.

ABOVE:
The girls of 4C at Gaywood Park show off the results of their cookery lesson in 1955.

RIGHT:
In 1954 the St James Boys football team are the proud winners of the King's Lynn primary shield, having regained it from Gaywood primary.

St James Boys school, in Hospital Walk, opened on 12th January 1932.

The following 2½ pages show the High School girls of 1955. Since the long photos are impossible to print on one page and be viewable, I have scanned the photo in sections (in this case, five photos make up one long one). The school originally opened in 1887 at 11, King Street and then moved in 1902 to (what was referred to as) the Trenowath Building. The school finally vacated the site in September 1979 when it amalgamated with Alderman Catleugh to form Springwood High School.

24

BELOW: The High School hockey team of 1959.

62518
RAS

Tennyson Avenue crossing, Summer 1955. For two weeks there was a rail strike by the ASLEF union. ASLEF was the union to which most footplate men (drivers & firemen) belonged. However, some footplate men belonged to the NUR, who were not on strike.

LEFT:
The train departing for Hunstanton is being driven by a NUR driver, who gives a two fingered salute to the ASLEF men at the gates. The outcome of the strike was that the drivers got a pay rise while the firemen got nothing!

BELOW:
After the strike, and on the same engine, Dennis Walker reprises the same salute to the cameraman.
The engine was performing shunting duties with carriage stock and stands beside the imposing signal gantry.

62518

62614
RAS

68495

ABOVE:
In the same year, Harry Ellis poses on the footplate of a class D16/3 passenger locomotive - in this case the specially maintained locomotive used for hauling the Royal train, mainly from Lynn to Wolferton and back.
Every 'Royal' journey would result in the driver receiving a new 10 shilling note in an envelope - the fireman would receive half a crown (2/6^d).

RIGHT:
Taking a break between shunting duties on the dock are Albert Johnson (shunter), Pat Collins (driver) and Tom Webb (mate).
The dock branch was about ¾ mile long and served the Alexandra (built 1869) and Bentinck (built 1883) docks.

TOP: In January 1956 The Queen visited the Grammar School on its 50th anniversary. Head boy David Fleming presents the Queen with a walnut jewel box made in the woodwork room.
ABOVE: 1956 The Grammar School's jazz band gave a concert in the town hall in aid of Hungarian relief.

TOP: 1956. Chapel Street looking north, near the corner with Norfolk Street. The businesses shown are Edward Towler, hairdresser (No.3), Laidlow's second-hand shop (No.5), Arthur Clarke, butcher & poultry (No.7), A Hutson, sewing machine dealer (No.9) & Gladys Turner, general grocer (No.11). Dennis & Son, pork butcher & provision merchant is just beyond Surrey Street.

ABOVE: 1956. St James Street. No.4 on the extreme right (partial view) is RG Errington (tailor), soon to change hands and become HW Peak Ltd. Next door (No.6) is The Chocolate Box run by the Misses Westwood, No.8 is George Bowers' butchers, No.10 is Miss Stokeley tobacconist, No.12 is Bensley's of Gaywood, cycle dealers - by 1960 Bensley's had taken over No.10 to include radio & TV. The Three Pigeons pub is in its last year of trading.

TOP: King's Lynn Technical College (commonly referred to as 'The Tec') was based at Hospital Walk and in the mid fifties, when this picture was taken, shows a group of domestic science students with staff. The man in the front middle was the principal Dr. Fox. ABOVE: Another photo taken at the same time with an engineering group.

The college was opened in 1894 by the Duke of York. It had cost £3000 to build and had a 100 seat lecture theatre, a physics lab, cookery room, chemistry lab, art room along with other class rooms. There was also a detached building housing a workshop for engineering. There was an overall capacity for 250 students.

The Corn Exchange was the main large venue in town. This picture (RIGHT) was taken in 1952. Traditionally it served its original purpose allowing farmers to trade.

It was also a centre of entertainment.:
MIDDLE LEFT:
In 1956 fans meet Lita Rosa (centre of picture) the singer with Ted Heath and His Music - the most successful of all the British bands.
MIDDLE RIGHT:
Ted Heath poses with fans at the same time.
BOTTOM:
In January 1960 a jiving contest took place at the Juke Box Jamboree. Here the winners, Ronnie Farrow & Glenda Tritt, show how it's done.

31

1958 Gaywood Park Girls.

Another long photo cut into five sections and spread over the next 2½ pages.

ABOVE: Summer 1956 at Gaywood Park Boys. The names, I believe, are
Back row left to right: Barry Gaskin, ? Davis, ?, Roger Booth, Andy Bone, Derek Wenner, Vic Troughton & Keith Branham.
Middle row: Michael Bray, Roger Oliver, Sonny Yallop, Gordon Bowering, Tony Aldous, Lou Donald, Doug Empson & Maurice Bunton.
Front row: Tony Anderson, Peter Langford, David Luther, ?, Barry Lilley, Peter Farmer & Peter Goldsmith.

TOP: Tower Street corner in 1957. Wheelers began trading in 1954. Next to Wheelers is Bear's Corn Stores. The Rummer pub was kept by Jack & Betty Cherrington. Diagonally opposite the Rummer was WH Johnson & Sons (ABOVE).
This was the premier garage in King's Lynn, being agents for Rolls Royce & Bentley among other well known makes of car. This photo was taken in 1959, a year after the business had been sold to Mann Egerton.

TOP RIGHT: A view looking up an empty St James Street towards Johnson's & the Rummer taken about 1959.

TOP LEFT: Further down the street was HW Peak Ltd. (Electrical goods, TV, radio & records) which can be seen next to Pratt & Coldham (hairdressers) on the corner of Church Street. The Watch Shop (page 6) had originally occupied the corner.

ABOVE: In this picture, (taken in 1957) the girls in the record department (Valerie Bacon & Ann Bocking) file new Christmas stock.

ABOVE: North Street in 1958. Two women walk from Pilot Street to St Ann's Street past E Southgate's provision merchants. The late morning sun streams through True's Yard and Watson's Yard.

BELOW: A year or two later and the side of the street (south side) the women walked down has disappeared, only True's Yard remains (out of view to the left of the cameraman).

RIGHT:
Pilot Street in 1958.
The sign directing heavy
traffic to the docks hangs
from the Methodist North
End Mission.
A lone cyclist has come
from Austin Street, turned
into Chapel Lane which
was (and still is) at the top
end of Pilot Street.
A van is parked beside
St Nicholas school building
(by this time a shoe
factory).

Chapel Lane and Pilot
Street were (and still are)
cobbled.

BOTTOM:
St Ann's Street in 1959.
Everybody knew Harry
Southgate, who sold
virtually everything a
modern supermarket does -
only in 5% of the space.
Not only a grocers but also
a post office. You never
needed to venture outside
North End - along with one
or two more shops in Pilot
Street, they stocked all you
needed and more!
The shop had been owned
by James Burrell before as
a grocer, baker
and post office.

The row of
property to the
right of the
shop is St
Ann's Fort (or
The Fort), and
behind that
was Burrell's
Yard (ref.
King's Lynn in
the 1930s).
Up until the
1920s my
father's family
lived at 6, St
Ann's Fort
when they then
moved to 6,
Chapel Lane.

TOP:
At 21, Blackfriars Street was Cozen's Hotel (seen here in 1959). Referred to as 'the temperance hotel' because no alcoholic drinks were served, it was a favourite with travelling salesmen who used to smuggle their own drink in, despite the watchful eye of the staff! The garage entrance can be seen at the right of the property and there was further access from Waterloo Street.

BOTTOM:
Townsend's corner bus-stop (1959), passengers catch an afternoon bus to Newlyn (39A). The Crystal Palace pub is on the corner of Marshall Street. Just out of view to the left of the picture was the Barley Mow pub.

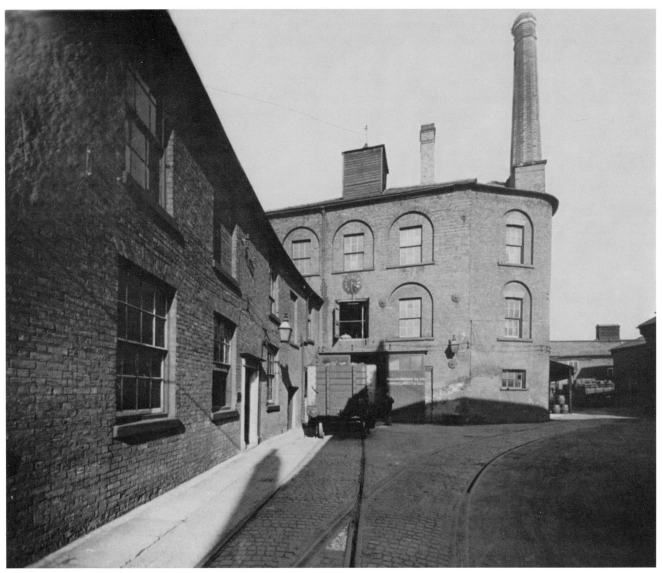

ABOVE: Morgan's Ladybridge brewery founded c1820, dominated the south side of Stonegate Street. The picture (looking east) above (probably mid fifties) shows another spur off the harbour branch rail network inside the brewery yard where the late afternoon sun casts shadows across the yard.

LEFT: This picture (1962) taken from the junction of Church Street & Stonegate Street shows the newer bottling plant on the right. The brewery was demolished in the late sixties to make way for Hillington Square.

A new industry at West Lynn

LEFT:

In October 1951 the Lynn News announced the opening of Fropax on the west bank of the river (nowadays usually referred to as the Donald Cook's site).

The caption for the picture stated:

'Green capped and aproned employees of Fropax, new quick-freeze factory at West Lynn, pick over spinach leaves for processing'. This was experimental work into what is today a multi-million pound business.

The firm planned to go into full scale production in the following year, with first of the season's freezable produce - asparagus. About 150 local people would be involved, the paper stated.

Fropax 1959

ABOVE:
The photo above looks like a case of 'too many chiefs' - but maybe they are trying to overcome the problem of there being more peas on the floor than on the conveyor belt.
With four managers watching it probably makes the workers very nervous!

LEFT:
Staff sort the bad from the good.

ABOVE LEFT:
A popular pub in the 50s was the Duke of Fife on the Saturday Market Place. It was run by an ex footballer called 'Taffy' Williams. It was often the meeting place for friends before moving on to other venues in town.
The two photos (taken in the 'Spanish Bar') above show and from left to right: Bernard 'Blackie' Allan, unknown man with glasses, Ronnie Farrow, Michael 'Dolly' Dolman and Lennie Farrow.
ABOVE RIGHT: From left to right: George Randall, 'Yacca' Yates, John Fish and 'Sly' Fretwell.
I believe that John Fish went on to be Jimmy Savile's minder.
BELOW:
The Saturday Market Place in 1967. From the left is Maude's Ltd. (credit drapers & general outfitters), Prior's butchers, Duke of Fife (which had been closed since October 1965 when the licence was transferred to the new pub on the Fairstead), Eva Baird (antiques), Crisp's Chemist , Barrett & Co. launderers, dyers & cleaners and Court Bros. (furnishers).

The South Quay

ABOVE:

The date of the picture above is thought to be 1959 or possibly early 60s.

The Kathe Ahrens is unloading its cargo into a lorry.

LEFT:

This picture shows part of the extensive rail network which ran from Harbour Junction to the Purfleet.

The last locomotive to run down the quay was in 1955 - after that any shunting of wagons was done using a tractor. The shunting of wagons ceased in 1968.

The South Quay had been rebuilt in 1954.

In January 1970 the two wrought iron swing bridges over the Millfleet and the Nar were demolished, thus severing forever the track along the quay - and also cutting off a short cut to town for South Lynners!

In the middle right background can be seen the two cranes on the Boal Quay and, in the far background, the 'muck works' dominates the horizon.

RIGHT:
The Boal Quay in the mid-late fifties.
Originally known as the Boll Quay (from
Boll - an old word meaning a measure of
weight & capacity) was first mentioned in
the 15th century.
The quay pictured was reconstructed in 1927
when the two cranes were installed.
Raw materials for the 'muck works' or more
correctly West Norfolk Fertilisers (WNF)
were unloaded here. The materials would
then make the short journey along the
harbour branch-line to the WNF sidings.
The materials included iron pyrites, and coal
for the older 'lead chamber' process and
sulphur for the more modern 'contact'
process. Other materials inwards included
phosphate, muriate of potash and sulphate
of ammonia.
Spent ore from the chamber process was
shipped out. The carriage of materials was
done using 16 ton open-topped wagons.

Beyond the Boal Quay in the picture is the
South Quay.

BELOW:
A view of WNF from Bunnett Avenue in the
early sixties.
It used to be said that if you lived in South
Lynn the chances were that you worked at
WNF, Cooper's or on the railway.
The 'muck works' had started production in
1872.

44

TOP:
Occupying a area between 125 & 161 Saddlebow Road was the West Norfolk Fertilisers. This aerial view of the works was taken in 1953. As a boy, in the early fifties, I remember cycling past the works and seeing the acidic brown fumes of nitrogen dioxide escaping into the atmosphere.

ABOVE:
Two ships with cargoes of phosphate in the process of being unloaded on the Boal quay in the early 1960s.

RIGHT:
Near the end of Saddlebow Road was the Station Hotel - in 1953 the landlord was the well-known ex-international footballer, Jack Howe.

BELOW:
100 yards or so further on was South Lynn station, seen here in 1957. South Lynn was at the heart of the old M&GN railway which ran from beyond Bourne and Peterborough in the west to Gt. Yarmouth in the east.
By now, part of British Railways, it was only two years from closure.

The picture shows the Push-Pull (South Lynn to King's Lynn shuttle) leaving the station for the short trip to King's Lynn station. To save having to run the locomotive round the train on its return, the driver could operate the locomotive from the rear carriage. Here the driver is just visible as he leaves the station.

1960 saw the 3 millionth Mini roll off the production line. The LASER was developed. The Magnificent 7 was showing at the Majestic. Doc Martens mod boots (called 1460) were in the shops. Lonnie Donegan sang 'My old man's a dustman' and Roy Orbison had a hit with 'Only the Lonely'. Fairy Liquid was introduced.

In 1961 the Avengers first appeared on the TV. Breakfast at Tiffanys was on at the Pilot. Scalextric was all the rage. The first E Type Jag was produced. Private Eye was launched. The Twist was the new dance thanks to Chubby Checker.

1962. The Polaroid camera was on sale. Z Cars and The Saint appeared on television. The Shadows (Wonderful Land) seemed to be No.1 forever, while Cliff Richard sang about 'The Young Ones'. The most popular record on the Whisky jukebox was Gene Chandler's 'Duke of Earl'. Embassy cigarettes were introduced.

In 1963 The Beatles had their first No.1 (From Me To You). The Mersey sound was dominating the charts (Billy J Kramer and Gerry & The Pacemakers both had No.1's in this year. Dr. Who and Steptoe & Son were seen on TV. The 'Great train robbery' and the 'Profumo' affair (Christine Keeler & Mandy Rice Davies) dominated the news headlines this year.

1964 saw Pirate radio hit the airways with Radio Caroline & Radio London - operating from a safe distance out in the North Sea. The Majestic was showing 'A Hard Day's Night' and 'Mary Poppins'. while on television we first watched Top of the Pops, The Likely Lads & Play School. The Searchers 'Needles & Pins' and Sandie Shaw '(There's) Always Something There to Remind Me' were big hits.

1965 - all dedicated followers of fashion headed for Carnaby Street to the sounds of 'Ticket to Ride' and 'I Got You Babe' (incidentally one of the fastest selling singles in Lynn ever). Winston Churchill died - how we need a leader like him now. Over 8 million people owned a car by now. 'The Man from UNCLE' first appeared on TV in this year.

The Beach Boys had 'Good Vibrations' in 1966 while The Stones sang 'Paint it Black'. Mini skirts arrived in Lynn but for some boys 'Action Man' was more exciting. Football fever hit everyone when England won the World Cup.

1967 saw the introduction of the microwave - a boon for all us culinary challenged males! The Prisoner and Trumpton were first shown on TV, along with The Monkees. Colour TV was first shown on BBC2. 'A Whiter Shade of Pale' proved to be another phenomenal seller in the town's record shops. Che Guevara (whose silhouette poster appeared on every rebel's bedroom wall) was killed. This year was known as the 'summer of love' but, to most of us, it was no different to any other year in the 60s! 'Sergeant Pepper' was released and the BeeGees had their first hit.

In 1968 we listened to The Beatles Hey Jude and Louis Armstrong's Wonderful World. Television showed us Hawaii Five-0 and Dad's Army made its first appearance. Martin Luther King was shot. The Ford Anglia was phased out and the Escort was introduced.

1969 saw the first man on the moon while Star Trek coincidentally first appeared on TV. Butch Cassidy & The Sundance Kid was on at the Majestic. This was the year that saw the introduction of mammography to detect breast cancer. There was Woodstock in America. Concorde first flew. BBC1 and ITV first screened colour. Harry Worth was popular throughout the decade.

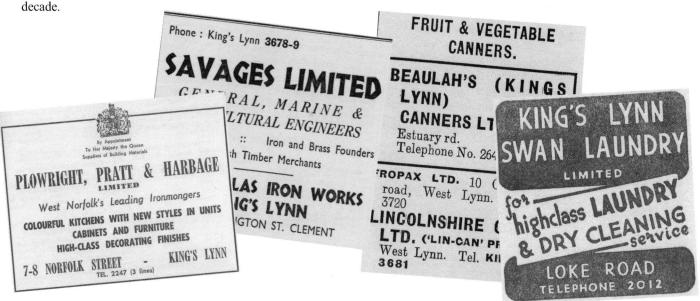

1950	1970
From 7 Saturday Mkt. place to Tuesday Mkt. Place	**From 7 Saturday Mkt. place to Tuesday Mkt. Place**
East Side	*East Side*
1 Williamson, Donald E	1 Smith A. jeweller
2 Kettering & Leicester Boot Co. Ltd	2 Kettering & Leicester Boot Co.Ltd
3 Hamblin Theodore Ltd. Dispensing opticians	3 Fairtax Travel Agency
4a Lown & Capps, printers	4a Lown & Capps, printers
4 Barrett CG & Co Ltd. Launderers, dyers & cleaners	4 Barnard S (Confectioner)
5 Hartley GM Ltd. Ladies & childrens outfitters & general drapers	5 Carters, domestic appliances, TV & radio dealers
6 Hartley GM Ltd. Ladies & childrens outfitters & general drapers	6 Tesco, grocers
7 Hartley GM Ltd. Ladies & childrens outfitters & general drapers	7 Tesco, grocers
8 Cheshire Cheese P.H. Horace G King	8 Sketchley Ltd. dry cleaners
9 Easters (Radio Services) Wireless engineers	9 Crown Wallpapers
10 to 16 Jermyn & Sons Ltd. Departmental Store	10 to 16 Jermyn & Sons Ltd. Departmental Store
here is Union Lane	**here is Union Lane**
17 Heath & Heather Ltd. Health food stores	17 Wheelers (Tower St. Corner Ltd), television dealers
17a Dickson, Nellie. Ladies hairdresser	17a Smith James & Son (Cleaners) Ltd
	17b, Gordon, ladies' hairdresser
18 Turner W & E. Ltd. Boot makers	18 Turner W & E. Ltd. Boot makers
19 Murdochs, pianoforte manufacturers	19 Abbey National Building Society
20 Lennards Ltd. Boot makers	20 Lennards Ltd. Boot makers
21/ 22 Le Grice Bros. Ltd. Fashions, fabrics & general drapery	21/22
24 & 25 Hepworths Ltd. Clothiers	24 & 25 Hepworths Ltd. Clothiers
here is Sedgeford Lane	**here is Sedgeford Lane**
26 Hiltons Ltd. Boot makers	26 Hiltons Ltd. Boot makers
here is New Conduit Street	**here is New Conduit Street**
34 Foster Bros Clothing Co. Ltd. Outfitters	34 Foster Bros Clothing Co Ltd Outfitters
35 London Central Meat Co. Ltd.	35
36 Barratt W.& Co. Ltd. Boot makers	36 Stylo, Boot makers
37 Star Supply Stores, grocers	37 Fenton Harry Ltd. Outfitters
38 Benefit Footwear Ltd. boot & shoe dealers	38 Benefit Footwear Ltd. boot & shoe dealers
38a Maypole Dairy Co. Ltd. grocers	39
39, 40 & 41 Ladyman JH & Co Ltd. Grocers & provision merchants, wines & spirits & The Gallery Restaurant & Café.	40
	41
42 Hipps Ltd. tailors	42 International Tea Co.'s Stores Ltd. grocers
43 & 44 Boots The Chemists	43 & 44 Boots The Chemists
45 Queen's Head P.H. Jack Tozer	45 Perkins Dorothy Ltd. ladies' outfitters
46 East Anglian Trustee Savings Bank	46 Freeman, Hardy & Willis Ltd. Boot makers
47 Freeman, Hardy & Willis Ltd. Boot makers	47 Freeman, Hardy & Willis Ltd. Boot makers
48 & 49 Goddard George Ltd. Outfitters, hatters & hosiers	48 & 49 Goddard George Ltd. Tailors
50 Woodcock A .B. Ltd. bakers	50 Woodcock A. B. Ltd. bakers
51 Rivetts of Lynn, Drapers	51 Rivetts of Lynn, Ladies' outfitters
52 Gallyon & Sons Ltd. Guns & fishing tackle & sports outfitters	52 Gallyon & Sons Ltd. Gun makers
53 Finlay & Co. Ltd. Tobacconists	53 Finlay & Co. Ltd. Tobacconists
	53a Smith Jas. & Son (Cleaners) Ltd
54 Mann, Egerton & Co.Ltd. Electrical Engineers	54 Modelia, Costumiers
55 Allen & Neale (Chemists) Ltd	55 Allen & Neale (Chemists) Ltd
here is Norfolk Street	**here is Norfolk Street**
56 Briggs & Co. Ltd. Boot makers	56 Briggs & Co. Ltd. Boot makers
56a Robinson Molly, ladies' hairdresser	56a Bateman's, ophthalmic opticians
57 Marks & Spencer Ltd. Bazaar	57 Marks & Spencer Ltd. Department store
58 Marks & Spencer Ltd. Bazaar	58 Marks & Spencer Ltd. Department store
59 Marks & Spencer Ltd. Bazaar	59 Marks & Spencer Ltd. Department store
60 Marks & Spencer Ltd. Bazaar	60 Marks & Spencer Ltd. Department store
61 Sketchley Dye Works, dyers & cleaners	61 Sketchley Ltd. dry cleaners
61a London Kiosks Ltd. tobacconists	
62 Williams Miss Marjorie. Gowns	62 Eve. Gowns
63 Midland Bank Ltd.	63 Midland Bank Ltd
here is Surrey Street	**here is Surrey Street**

These two pages compare the owners of the High Street properties as at 1950 and 1970.
There are many other businesses operating above some of the shops.
Where possible (space permitting) the shop names and their wares have been copied as read from Kelly's directories.
Note, in some cases, the change of description of a business over the 20 years (M&S is a bazaar in 1950!).
In 1950 Woolworth's occupied Nos.73 & 74 but by 1970 had expanded to include No.75.

1950	1970
From Tuesday Mkt. Place to 7 Saturday Mkt. Place	**From Tuesday Mkt. Place to 7 Saturday Mkt. Place**
here is Surrey Street	**here is Surrey Street**
West Side	*West Side*
65 Jones & Dunn, outfitters.	65 Jones & Dunn, outfitters, tailors & hatters
66 Walton Bros. (King's Lynn & Hunstanton) Ltd. Gents outfitters	66 Walton Bros. (King's Lynn & Hunstanton) Ltd. Gents outfitters
67 Swain Ernest E. photographer	67 King's Lynn Camera Centre, photographers
68	68 Eastern Gas
69 Targett PS & Daughter. Stationers & Newsagents	69 Broughall W.H.Ltd. Shoe repairers
70 Samuel H. Ltd. Jewellers	70 Samuel H. Ltd. Jewellers
71 Peatling Thos & Sons Ltd. wine & spirit merchants	71 Peatling & Cawdron Ltd. wine & spirit merchants.
72 Kirk, Robert. boot & shoe dealer	72 Kirk R. & Son Ltd. shoe dealers
73 & 74 Woolworth FW & Co. Ltd. Departmental store	73/74 Woolworth F.W.& Co. Ltd. Departmental store
75 Joys (A. H. Emons Ltd.), Costumiers	75 Woolworth F.W.& Co. Ltd. Departmental store
76 Greenlees & Sons (" Easiephit " Footwear) Ltd	76 Greenlees & Sons (" Easiephit "Footwear) Ltd
77 Rivetts of Lynn, wool stores	77 Rivetts, wool shop
78 Solesta Ltd. Costumiers	78 Dolcis Shoe Co. Ltd
79 Norfolk News Co. Eastern Daily Press	79 Norfolk News Co. Eastern Daily Press
80 King W J. Jeweller	80 Purdy W. Ltd. Bakers
81 Burlingham S Ltd. Jewellers & Silversmiths	81 Burlingham S Ltd. Jewellers, Watch & Clockmakers
here is Library Court	**here is Library Court**
81a & 81b Burlingham & Lloyd Ophthalmic opticians	81a Burlingham & Lloyd Ltd. ophthalmic opticians.
82 Currys Ltd. Cycle dealers	82 Currys Ltd. Electrical appliances
83 Joy's (A H Emons Ltd). Costumiers	83 Fields Henry Ltd. Ladies' outfitters
84 Goodchild P M & Son Ltd. Photographers	84 Woodhouse Jas. (Furnishers) Ltd. House furnishers
85 Rose John & Son. Leather goods & sports outfitters	85
86 Emmerson & Youngman, hairdressers	86
87 Hepworth GA & Co Ltd. Costumiers	87 Lyons, Costumiers
88 Cambridge & King's Lynn Belfast Linen Warehouse Co.	88 Belfast (The), linen drapers.
89 Speed & Son Ltd. (Watchmakers & Jewellers).	89 Speed & Son Ltd. Watchmakers, jewellers & silversmiths
90 Fleming, Reid & Co. Ltd. Scotch wool stores	90 Stead & Simpson Ltd. Shoe makers
91 to 97 Scott & Son (King's Lynn) Ltd. House furnishers	91 to 97 Scott & Son (King's Lynn) Ltd. House furnishers
here is Purfleet Street	**here is Purfleet Street**
98 & 99 Inland Revenue, Collector of Taxes	98/99 H.M. Customs & Excise
	98/99 Andre, ladies' hairdresser
98 & 99 Burton Montague Ltd. Tailors	98 & 99 Burton Montague Ltd. Tailors
99a Fletcher W & E Ltd. Butchers	99a Fletcher W & R Ltd. Butchers
100 Greig David Ltd. Provision dealers	100 Greig David Ltd. Provision dealers
101 Brown Bros. & Taylor Ltd. House furnishers	101
102 Fell S. & Sons Ltd. Cycle dealers	102 Bellmans, wool stores
103 International Tea Co. Stores Ltd. Grocers	103 Poysers, card shop
103a Hole Jane. Children's Outfitter	103a Barclays Bank Ltd
103b Hunters the Teamen Ltd. Grocers	103b Mac Fisheries Ltd. fishmongers
here is Baker Lane	**here is Baker Lane**
104 Broughton Stanley C. fruiterer	104 Devantier Carpets
105 Hamson Jsph. Clothier	105 Etam Ltd. Ladies' outfitters
106 Hamson Jsph. Jeweller	106 Willerby Tailoring Ltd
107 Home & Colonial Stores, grocers	107
108 Winton-Smith F Ltd. Ham & beef dealers	108 Co-operative Cleaners Ltd
109 Hollywood Hats (Marshall & Knight Ltd) Milliners	109
110 Fifty Shilling Tailors (Prices Tailors Ltd)	110 Collier J. tailor
111 Lipton Ltd. Provision merchants	111 Granada, television rental
112 Palmer & Harvey Ltd. wholesale, Adcocks tobacconists	112 Palmer & Harvey Ltd. Tobacconists
113 Salter & Salter Ltd. Boot dealers	113
114 Bennell F. W. & Son, bakers	114
114a Wigram & Ware Ltd. Opticians	114a Gardenia, restaurant
115 & 117 Richard Shops Ltd. Costumiers	115 & 117 Richard Shops Ltd. costumiers
118 Ebling Frank, fancy goods dealer	118 Coxheads, television rental
119 Pugh & Sons. Hosiers & Footware specialists	119 D.E.R. television rental.
120 Barnards, fruiterers	120 Matthes Ltd. Bakers
121	121
122 London Central Meat Co. Ltd. Butchers	122
123 Wenn's Commercial Hotel	123 Wenn's Hotel

ABOVE: In 1959 M&S bought the vacated garage site which had been owned by Mann Egerton at 145, Norfolk Street in order to expand. By 1960 (when this picture was taken) their expansion plans were well under way.

They had previously expanded in the thirties when they took over 58, Norfolk Street (Benjamin Hardy's ironmongers) & 59, Norfolk Street (EG Millett clothiers). Their original shop was 57, Norfolk Street.

TOP: The end of steam in King's Lynn - ironically a locomotive is pulling down the engine shed in unceremonious fashion in 1960.
BOTTOM: A class 31 diesel locomotive is about to leave Campbell's siding and join the London line at Harbour Junction to head south to Ely and then onward north (via Whitemoor yard, March) to Scotland, carrying the one millionth can of soup in 1961. Sometimes if this regular service (known as the 'soup train') was late on departure it would then be routed via Wisbech (leaving the London line at Magdalen Road junction) in order to make its connection at Whitemoor with a train for the north.

TOP: New Conduit Street in 1960. ABOVE: New Conduit Street in 1961. DER have recently moved into No.3, which had been vacated by the Regal Café On the other side of the street, Custance (tailors) have moved into what was Horner's music shop. The iron railings just before Custance is the Congregational Church.

TOP LEFT: Nos.1 & 2 Broad Street in 1961. By the following year, Eastman's (butchers) & Miss J Flatt (greengrocer) had been replaced by the Whisky À Go-Go. At the end of Paradise Parade was the Cattle Market.

TOP RIGHT: Further along Broad Street was the well-known Market Fish Café owned by Jack Hillard.

LEFT: Another view of Broad Street looking towards the Post Office. On the left of the picture is JW Slator & Sons (ironmongers), owned at this time by WH King.

BOTTOM: This view (1961) was taken from Paradise Parade looking towards Baxter's Plain. The Broad Street Chambers building is now occupied by Maison Andreé hairdressers. Across Baxter's Plain is the Essex & Suffolk Insurance Co. Ltd. which had been Custance (tailors) previously.

ABOVE: Barclays Bank in 1955, just before its rebuilding, which took place over two years. The portico with the flat terrace roof supported by four ionic columns was removed from the front as part of the rebuilding.

MIDDLE LEFT
The Theatre Royal.
This was built in 1938 and was the third to be erected on this site - the previous two had been destroyed by fire.
The last picture to be shown was 'The Young Ones' on 14th April 1962.

BOTTOM LEFT
In 1962 the Theatre became the Alpha Bingo Club.
It then became the Mecca Bingo Club.

On bingo nights we used to have a quiet game of scrabble in the Rummer - that was until the bingo interval when the bar was thrown into complete mayhem as the 'bingo crowd' fought to get a drink before the second half began.

Nos. 1&2 Broad Street.
TOP:
A full view of the Whisky (mid-late sixties), to the left is Broad Street and to the right Paradise Parade, leading to the Cattle Market.
RIGHT:
The interior of the Whisky showing the counter area - the jukebox was to the right behind the photographer.

The Whisky had opened in 1962. Arthur Richardson had seen a café in Wardour Street in Soho (called The Whisky a Go-Go) and decided to bring a little bit of Soho to Lynn. A Gaggia coffee machine produced Espresso coffee and by using trendy cups & saucers and installing a modern juke box he produced a magnet for younger people.

The name 'Whisky a Go-Go' was originally coined in the south of France by the man who also gave the name and concept to the term 'discothèque'. The best known Whisky in Sunset Strip, America actually came two years later in 1964.

The Tuesday Market Place.

TOP RIGHT: 1960. Customers mull over the wares on this stall near the Duke's Head. The stucco facade of the hotel is evident - this covers the original brick fascia.

BOTTOM RIGHT: The market has a great appeal, especially to people in the out-lying villages, when they would come in by the bus-load. In the last few years there has been a dramatic reduction in the size of the market. This is possibly because many of the traders now prefer more permanent shop locations within the town.

LEFT: An aerial view taken in the mid fifties shows the market place full (and the camera has caught only half of the stalls in its lens) - today it only occupies about a quarter of the market square.

Alderman Catleugh school 1961. The school had opened in September 1957 - although the official opening ceremony was held on 21st March 1958. This photo was taken of Mrs Gostling's needlework class showing off their own creations at a fashion show.
Back row: Gill Stebbings, ?, Janet Williamson, ?, ?, Linda Thompson, ?, Elizabeth Lawton, Ann Frankham, ?.
Front row: Vivienne Deacon, Dawn Pegg, Tessa Thompson, Moira ?, June Lemmon, ?,Ruth Watts.

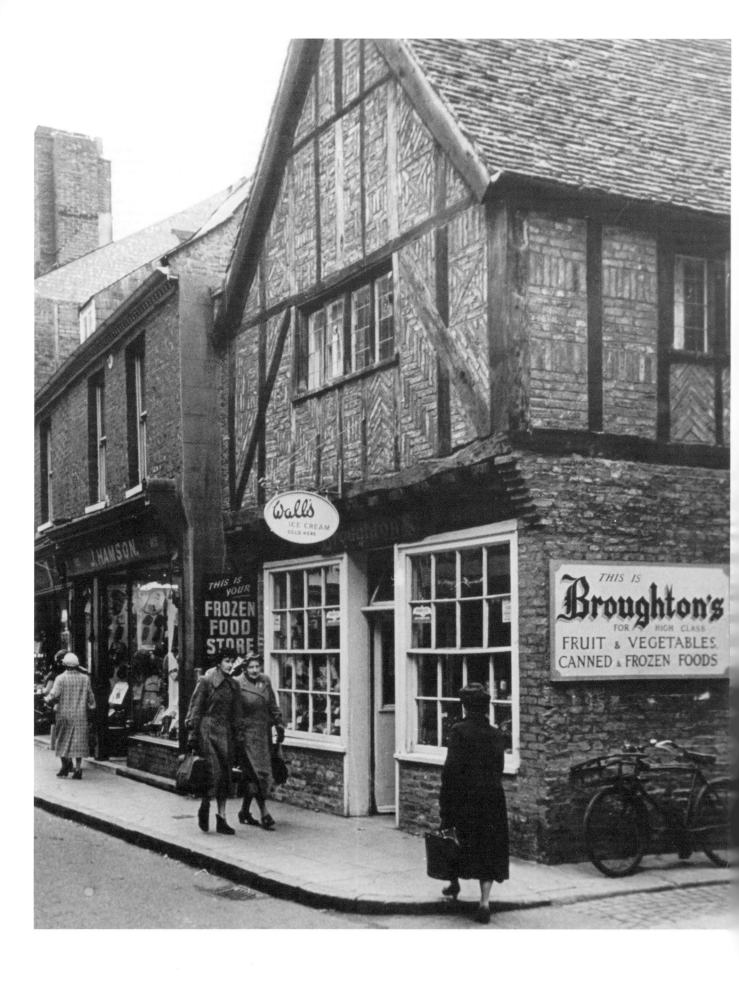

ABOVE: In 1960 Broughton's fruiterers, florists & frozen foods stood beside Baker Lane. Unfortunately this lovely old building (although not genuine Tudor) stood in the way of progress and has now been replaced by a 'modern' building .

TOP: The Cattle Market in August 1960 (looking towards Railway Road). The bus station and Sainsbury's & multi-storey car park now occupy this site.

In the fifties livestock was herded to and from the railway station across Railway Road and down Wellesley Street on Tuesdays - market day (this was generally a messy procedure for obvious reasons!).

ABOVE: A view of Montague Burton's in 1962. The New Conduit Street sign is affixed to the toilet block at the top of that street.

ABOVE: A new quay was built in the fisher fleet in 1960. Here it is nearing completion.
BOTTOM LEFT: Two years later the Gladys (built by the Worfolk Brothers) returns from a successful shrimping trip in The Wash.
BOTTOM RIGHT: The shrimps are still being cooked as the Gladys ties up. Albert Pegg is cooling the cooked shrimps.

King Edward V11 Grammar School 1960.
This long photo starts at the left-hand end (TOP) and extends over the next 2 ½ pages.

TOP:
The right-hand end of the 1960 Grammar School long photo.

LEFT:
The mayor and mayoress Mr & Mrs F Jackson have a guard of honour by Brownies as they enter St James Girls school from Paxton Terrace in 1960.

BELOW:
It's Christmas 1960 at St James Girls school in Paxton Terrace.

FW Woolworth & Co. Ltd. Occupied 73/75 Norfolk Street in 1962 when this staff photograph was taken in front of the shop. Until 1957 it occupied only 73 & 74 and, in that year, it took over 75 (Joy's costumiers). There are over 120 members of staff on in this photograph - most of whom would probably have been in full-time employment. The shop closed in 1985.

TOP: Bayes opened a second shop at 55, St James Street in 1957, into what was previously the Tower Café. A record department was installed upstairs, despite there being four other shops selling records in the town. In the fifties and sixties most record departments were within electrical/TV shops, and shops specialising in just records were only found in large cities.

On the first day of trading, the record department took only 1/3^d and that was for a middle to play a jukebox record someone had bought elsewhere! For the first three or four years the weekly takings were around £20 (£5 during the week & £15 on a good Saturday).

ABOVE: Here a customer is given help with a purchase. Getting a job in a record department was a plum job for school leavers. Those who worked with music were very enthusiastic, knew their product and had time for the customer.

These pictures were taken in December 1961.

TOP: In 1962, Lynn experienced its first taste of supermarkets when Elmo arrived at 112, Norfolk Street. Unfortunately, the picture was taken in the quiet of an evening and is very dark.

ABOVE: Ready to welcome customers - the interior of the shop.

TOP: Divers fine Foods Ltd (pictured in 1963) was at 7/9 Blackfriars Street.
ABOVE: Norfolk Street in 1963, looking towards Townsend's Corner. The Co-op (or The King's Lynn Working Men's Co-operative Society Ltd. to give it its full name) was opened in 1928. Just to the right of large hoarding is the entrance to Atto's Yard via Atto's Passage. The houses in this yard were pulled down in the pre-war town slum clearance (ref. King's Lynn in the 1930s).

TOP: High Street in 1963. Martin's Bank (left of picture) was 103a, Top Rank (TV rentals) was 103, Fell's (cycle dealers) was 102 and Weaver to Wearer (tailors) was at 101.
ABOVE: High Street in 1966 looking down towards Le Grice and WH Smith. Murdoch's music shop is now owned by Wheelers.

ABOVE Campbell's Finance department staff pose outside the office block in 1962.

BELOW Gaywood Park Girls pose with teacher Angela Cousins in the mid sixties.

TOP: Townsend's Corner in the early sixties. The end was near for K East, Dinkie (Mrs Ashwood), Andrews Chemist (who were about to move to the site at 39, Norfolk Street where the Sun Hotel once stood.) and the Co-op.

ABOVE: The Globe in 1962. Towards the rear of the building was the Palm Court dance hall. Further down Ferry Lane the hotel opened two more bars in the mid sixties - the Stable Bar and The River Bar. The Palm Court was popular with American servicemen and the local lads would meet them here to 'discuss' cultural differences.

LEFT:
A view from the upstairs of Briggs & Co. (boot makers) looking south down High Street in 1964.

BELOW
The suburbs of Lynn also had shops. In 1963 St Edmundsbury Road in North Lynn boasted a chemists (Bowskills), butchers (Masons), and a sizable grocers and post office (Co-op).

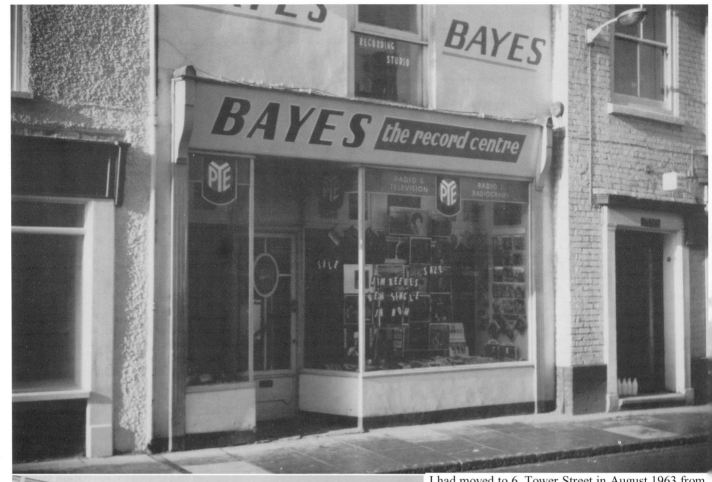

I had moved to 6, Tower Street in August 1963 from 55, St James Street in order to become independent and get a better trading position within the town.

ABOVE: In 1964 the record shop still shows signs of its previous use as a radio & television shop but by now it's the first record specialist shop in town - albeit a bit small.

Upstairs was the recording studio where most local bands recorded (sometimes several sessions) and even bands from as far away as Boston would come. From many of these sessions came records.

The tapes from the studio were sent away and varying quantities of records were ordered - usually 25 or 50. The records were sold in the shop and by the bands at their gigs. Since I programmed the Whisky jukebox I would put a copy on the box in order to get maximum coverage for the band and also sales through the shop.

MIDDLE LEFT:
On the evening of the 16th October 1964, Alan Drake and Tony Pull of the Sabres play in a recording session.

BOTTOM LEFT:
The band listen to a play back of the track.
The band in the picture are, from left to right:
Alan Drake, Tony Pull, Barry Leeder (aka Denny Raven), Pete Carter & Rick Meek.
Bands liked to sign their names on the studio wall - visible here are the signatures of the Tea Time Four & the Trojans.
In 1965 Janet joined me and for a while we ran the shop together (although she was on her own for times when I was teaching chemistry at the 'Tec'). Since we didn't have a kettle, she would get coffee from the Whisky - on a windy day we drank 'frothless' coffee!

ABOVE: Ladyman's was at 39, 40 & 41 High Street.
It's a lunch time in March 1964. A family study the menu at the RAC approved Gallery restaurant while a Salvation Army man collects for those less fortunate.
In the Kelly's of that year it stated that the business had been established over 150 years.

LEFT: At 48 & 49 High Street was George Goddard Ltd. After moving from here to the old Bird-in-Hand site in Norfolk Street for a few years it is now situated in Wellesley Street and is owned by WD Coe Ltd. of Ipswich.

Two more pictures of High Street in 1964.

ABOVE:

This shows the shops from New Conduit Street down to Ladyman's (off camera to the left). From Foster Bros (No.34), on the corner, the shops are: Baxters (No.35), W Barratt (No.36), International Stores (No.37), Benefit Footwear (No.38) and Maypole Dairy Co. (No.39). Oddly Kelly's gives Maypole the same street number as Ladyman's (39 to 41). Other references quote Maypole as 38a.

LEFT:

Looking to the left of Ladyman's, this is the view up High Street towards the Tuesday Market Place.

The other side of Boots is Dorothy Perkins formerly The Queen's Head, which was demolished in August 1960 in order to add another piece of sterile architecture to our High Street.

RIGHT:
The East Anglian Hotel in 1965. This was built c1850 shortly after the railway arrived in Lynn - the first trains ran in October 1846. The hotel stood on the corner of Blackfriars Road and Portland Street. Incorporated in the hotel (at the left of the building) was Barwell's off licence.
To the left of that are two large doors - it was from here that, on Sundays only, newspapers were sold. Beyond that was the Grey Friars Tavern (now The Fenman).
BELOW:
In 1965 the area of houses bounded by

Blackfriars Road, Coburg Street, Paxton Terrace and Wyatt Street (known as Lower Canada) was awaiting demolition. The larger building on the right was divided into two. The part on the corner was the Engineer's Tavern, whilst the left-hand part was my home, which was also owned by the brewery (Steward & Patterson). The door to the pub is in Coburg Street. The window partly boarded up in that street was the smoke room of the pub (see picture on page 11). On Saturday nights I would go to sleep to the sound of a piano sing-song from the pub. The shop had been run by Mrs L Ferlisi as a grocer's. It was very popular with the children from the school and all the local residents.

TOP: A diesel locomotive shunts across Tennyson Avenue in 1965. During the fifties the gates here, more often than not, were shut to road traffic as there was a continuous flow of goods wagons to sort. The passenger trains leaving Lynn were numerous, going to Hunstanton, Norwich (via Swaffham) London, Wisbech (via Magdelen Road) and to South Lynn to link with the old M&GN system for either Yarmouth or the Midlands. In the summer, motor traffic from the west (Peterborough etc.) had to go down Tennyson Avenue to get to Hunstanton and the North Norfolk coast - the result was total grid-lock through the town.

ABOVE: Gaywood Road crossing. An opportunist shot taken from my car one lunch time in 1967 shows a diesel multiple unit heading to the station from Hunstanton. The gates have been replaced by an automatic barrier. The line closed on 3rd May 1969.

ABOVE:
A view of Norfolk Street in 1965 taken from the corner of Chapel Street. On the left of the street can be seen Eastern Electricity (No.5 Norfolk St.), Plowright, Pratt & Harbage (Nos.7&8), Singer Sewing Machine Co. (No.9), Money's (No.10), Fiddaman's Hotel (No.11) & Nicholls & Campbell (Nos.11&12).

LEFT:
A view looking down the street 1967. On the left of the picture is Donaldson's fishmongers (No.141, Norfolk Street). Note their royal warrants above the shop awning. Both photos courtesy EDP.

TOP: Chapel Street in 1966, taken from the junction with Austin Street. The building behind the wall was the King's Lynn Labour Club premises (St. Augustines Club). This area was the site of an Augustinian (Black Friars) Priory. There is, still visible in Austin Street, a bricked up gateway to the Priory.

ABOVE: Looking in the opposite direction. The afternoon sun shines down Market Lane on the left, and just beyond, is the old Lattice House pub. In the 19th century there were over 20 pubs in the Chapel Street area. The only one to remain is the Lattice House.

Norfolk Street (looking towards Albert Street) in 1966. Melias Ltd. has closed. Another small grocer succumbing to the early effect of the supermarkets. Stratfords is on the left of the picture - one of the few high street names from this era still trading (2007). On reprinting this book Stratfords is no longer open in Norfolk Street (2011). If we'd had a good Saturday at the shop, Janet & I would treat ourselves to a Wimpy tea.

Another long school photo (over this and the next page), this time of The Convent junior school.
Taken in 1967 just three years before this junior section of the school was closed.

TOP: Norfolk Street October 1967 and Elmo has now become Finefare.

ABOVE: Broad Street in 1967. The businesses from the left of the picture are Witting Bros. (fruiterers & greengrocers), Crome & Sons (heating engineers), Cattle Market Tavern. The entrance to Baptist's Yard is next, then Mayes (second-hand dealer), Mrs Rye (fruiterer) before Bath's Yard, and finally Frost & Walsh (builders). At the end of the street is The Grosvenor. On the right of the street is the old Cattle Market, the old Electric Cinema which is, at this time, LE Taylor's garage, at the front of which is two shops - Myer Finkelblech (jewellers) and Ryder & Crosskill (confectioners) and at the end of the street is Catleugh's.

TOP: High Street looking south to the Saturday Market Place in the mid sixties.
BOTTOM: High Street from No.76 (Easiephit). The other side of the EDP office is Purdy's (bakers), and upstairs the coffee bar - another favourite meeting place.

Two pictures of the High School in 1967. TOP: The chemistry lab (which I believe was in the yard of the Guildhall).
ABOVE: Lunch time in the school canteen. This looks like civilised dining with a great view across the river.
Our school canteen was an old prefab with rows of tables overlooking Gaywood Road!

ABOVE: The Bentinck dock in the mid sixties. In the 1950s the quay where the ships are moored was widened so that three lines of rail wagons could be run down the quay. Six new Smith-Rodley electrically powered quay cranes were erected. Lynn in the sixties was primarily an importing port (and probably still is). All four vessels are unloading. The leftmost ship is still loaded with timber, ready for unloading. The next vessel has been unloaded (note the height of the vessel above the waterline). The third vessel is still fully loaded with timber ready to be unloaded. The fourth vessel (the Alster from Hamburg) has just unloaded plant and machinery packed in wooden crates - probably from Claas in West Germany. The pitched roofs of the Bristow & Copley sheds can be seen behind the first vessel.

ABOVE:
This is a picture of the Princess Margaret Quay, Alexandra Dock, taken in 1968.

The cranes were made by the Dutch firm of Figee. They had been installed in the 1930s and were, in fact, erected back to front to the way intended! Although of rather primitive design, they were easily maintained and even in the 1990s they were still serviceable, but had become redundant and thus dismantled.

The cars are early Skodas which were, at the time, all imported through Lynn.

It's hard to believe that the modern Bentleys are built by the same manufacturing group as Skodas.

LEFT:
Unloading timber on the Bentinck dock in the mid sixties.

ABOVE:
Union Street in 1967 from All Saints Street looking toward Coronation Square.
RIGHT: A view from the other end of the street. Just out of shot on the left of the picture is The Volunteer Stores pub. The property on the right was originally the Robin Hood pub. After the war it became a laboratory owned by Dr Russell Lankshear.
In September 1952 my first job was working here after school. The work was unpaid but I expected nothing as I was learning so much chemistry. 'Doc' was also a qualified engineer and, on Sunday mornings,

would give lectures on the workings of steam locomotives to railway staff at Lynn station. These dedicated railway men would give up their Sunday mornings to voluntarily attend the meetings. In a room at the back of the laboratory he also chaired meetings of the local Tory party. It was my job on such nights to get the room ready and light the paraffin stove - presided over by a large portrait of Winston Churchill!

ABOVE:
Austin Street looking east in 1960.
A Jermyn's van has just pulled up outside the Post Office Engineering department on the left of the picture.
These buildings were the original headquarters of the M&GN railway.
The M&GN office closed in 1936 when traffic administration was taken over by the LNER.

By 1960 the empty properties opposite the van had become unsafe and would be shortly cordoned off because there was a risk of falling tiles.
Further down the street on the right is Garland Yard (between 56 & 58). Just visible even further down (between 64 & 66) is the sign of Swarby Hire Car Co & Swarby School of Motoring.
This business was situated in Watling's Yard - referred to by some people at the time as Hasting's Yard.

RIGHT: Austin Street (in May 1961) looking west towards Chapel Street.
The old M&GN headquarters can be seen on the right of the picture. Next to this building is the entrance to George Booth's confectionery warehouse and 'pop' factory.
Just beyond, is the single storey shop of Hector Shaw (greengrocer). The sun streams down Albert Street (just beyond the motor bike).

RIGHT:
Broad Street in 1968 looking north. The end is nigh for the whole street including the Whisky.
Further up the street on the left is the derelict Empire Cinema.

BELOW:
The Empire Cinema, in 1962, is up for sale. It's been over thirty years since the last picture show.
Fly posters advertise 'The Story of Cinderella' performed by the King's Lynn Players at the Guildhall of St George. If that's not for you then there's always wrestling at the Corn Exchange.

The Empire had opened in 1913 and, after just 16 years, closed in 1929.
Unfortunately, the cinema had never been wired for sound so, with the advent of the 'talkies', it succumbed to a sudden demise. After that there was little demand for the hall except for the odd sale or exhibition.

TOP: Windsor Road in 1967. On the left two bicycles lean against a low wall next to Pett's (grocers). Further along, on the corner o Keppel Street is Gower (grocer) advertising Typhoo tea. Next to Gower's is Walker Anderson (ironmongers) and the other side o Victoria Street is TR Wagg (baker). On the right of the street is DH Wood (greengrocer), TR Richardson (butcher) and further alon; the Live & Let Live pub.

BOTTOM: Purfleet Street in 1967. Just beyond Scott's is the (now) empty Central Hotel. At the bottom of the street is the Lynn New: offices. On the left is Scott's warehouse. The street enjoyed fame when briefly featured in the 1965 film 'Operation Crossbow'.

ABOVE: South Clough Lane in 1968, looking west towards Tower Street. The general grocery shop on the corner of Regent Street is owned by Miss Lilian Lane. Within a short space of about 5 years the whole site had disappeared to make way for a car park.

LEFT:
The cameraman has moved up the street (ref. the white fronted (ex) shop on the right) and is standing next to the opening to Melbourne Street. On the corner is the Rose & Thistle pub whose landlord was Gordon Baker.
The alley on the right is Blackfriars Passage leading to Blackfriars Street.
The property next to the passage had been a Labour Party office in the early sixties. Blackfriars Street had originally been called North Clough Lane.

LEFT:
High Street 1968.
David Greig Ltd. (provision dealers) stands at
100, High Street and just beyond is W&R Fletcher Ltd. (butchers) at 99a, High Street.

Weaver to Wearer Ltd. (on the left in the picture) is offering £2/2s/0d (2 guineas) off if you order a made-to-measure suit.

BELOW: A view looking north down High Street in 1967.

INSET: A photo of the interior of Le Grice in 1967.

TOP: Tower Street looking north in 1960. By now the old skating rink has gone forever, having been demolished to make way for William H King's used car centre. Brookers (motor engineers & motor cycle agents) still trade - they were situated behind the Skating rink. Steve Morris' Model Shop is clearly visible.

BOTTOM: Tower Street looking south in 1966. Milton's (butchers) is to the left of the picture. The shop adjoining Milton's, which had been a confectioners in the early sixties, appears empty. Dryden's now occupy Nos. 1&2 Tower Street. In 1960 No.1 had been a florist. Next to Bayes (No.6), Terra Nova (No.8) has just opened - I wasn't going to see much of Janet from now on!

RIGHT:
An aerial view (taken in 1968) of the Fire Station, St. Edmund's School & Shell-Mex/BP depot. The depot, built in the mid 50s, mostly replaced an older site built in the 30s. At its busiest it handled 400,000 tons of oil products per year - all shipped via the Bentinck dock and involving about 250 ships - nearly all confined to arrive on spring tides (sometimes two or three ships in a 24 hour period). Half the through-put was for RAF stations in the region. The new northern bypass (top right of picture) is ready to be opened when the section to South Wootton is completed.

BELOW: An aerial view of the docks area in the mid sixties. The Alexandra is nearest to the river and the Bentinck is on the right of the picture. Clearly visible is the Fisher Fleet. Note the large network of railway tracks - sadly no longer used.

TOP: Coronation Square, 1968. The area is about to disappear forever. Crooked Lane led to Bridge Street and to the left was Union Street. To the right of the picture was Coronation Hall and a passage leading to the Millfleet.

BOTTOM: At the same time, a view from South Lynn Plain (at the end of Valingers Road) looking towards All Saints Street, which also leads to Bridge Street. The pub on the corner is the Anchor. The gap after AW Arrowsmith (butcher) is where 2 to 5 All Saints Street were (ref. King's Lynn in the 1930s). The large house to the left of Arrowsmiths is Welwick House. Welwick House was a Georgian building and was the first museum in the town. Lynn Society of Arts & Sciences took over the house in 1913. It contained a lecture room, readingroom and conversation room. By the 1950s it had fallen into disrepair and was demolished in 1969 to make way for the Hillington Square development.

ABOVE: It's the late sixties and workmen dig up the road on Baxter's Plain. At the beginning of the decade this area had still retained its cobbles. The cameraman has positioned himself upstairs at the Post Office. Within a year this scene looking down New Conduit Street will be gone forever as in August 1969 new units start to appear in the street.

The Essex and Suffolk Insurance Company's office had originally been the shop of Custance & Son (tailors). Custance had previously located from 88, High Street in 1926 and named these premises 'The Breeches House' since their business was ladies & gents tailors and riding breeches makers.

Demolition on this building began in December 1969.

BELOW LEFT: Custance had moved to 25, New Conduit Street at this time - into the old Horner's Ltd. Music shop. The Gothic arch doorway to the left of the shop leads to the Society of Friends (Plymouth Brethren) Meeting House.

BELOW RIGHT: The north side of Baxter's Plain, again in the late sixties and Joan Billings' (hairdressers) and the Norwich Building Society (which replaced the tobacconists & café) are still trading - just!

TOP: Townsend's Corner in 1963. Some shops are being demolished to make way for John Kennedy Road. Andrews the Chemist have already relocated to 39, Norfolk Street in a temporary shop on the site of the old Sun Hotel.

ABOVE:1969. Sedgeford Lane car park behind the Majestic. On the left of the photo is the prefabricated building that was (at different times in the fifties) known as the Tower Restaurant & British Restaurant. At this time it was used as a canteen by the High School. An early traffic warden patrols in a Fair Isle pullover.

ABOVE:
Mrs L Bocking ran the newsagents at 10, Stonegate Street on the corner of Church Street, opposite to HE George & Sons Ltd. (pork butchers).
In the summer of 1969 the shop was in the process of being re-decorated.
The business, which had suffered from loss of trade when the old brewery on the other side of the street had been demolished to make way for new housing , was beginning to improve thanks to residents moving into the new Hillington Square flats.

Unfortunately in August 1969 Mrs Bocking was threatened, bound & gagged and robbed by three masked men.
The lady, who was in her sixties, decided not to continue trading and retired in November of that year.

RIGHT:
Mrs Bocking sorts newspapers not long before finally retiring.

The number of nationwide recorded crimes in 1950 was 461,435
By 1969 this number had more than trebled to 1,488,638
By 1999 the number had gone up 11 fold to 5,109,089
Despite successive governments pledges, no-one has presided over anything like a substantial fall in these figures.

TOP: The entrance to Dodman's works on Gaywood Road in the late sixties. The Royal crest above the gate occasionally had to be removed to allow very tall fabrications to leave the works. Living in Lower Canada, I used to awake to the sound of the 7.25am hooter at the works. This was sounded to alert staff that they should be ready to start work. The hooter was sounded again at 7.30am - if any employee failed to clock on by 7.33am he would lose 15 minutes of pay.

BELOW: Boilers that were too wide to be taken by rail from Dodman's siding and had to be transported by road. Most transporters would turn left out of the gates and head for Townsend's Corner in order to travel up London Road to leave town. Traffic had to be stopped, especially at the turning from Norfolk Street into Railway Road.

The boilers were used by such firms as bakeries and dairies. The large tower (seen in the background) that dominated the Dodman works was a riveting tower.

Boilers (in their construction) were hauled vertically up the tower in order to rivet the various components together. This would involve man inside the boiler being supplied with a succession of extremely hot rivets. The rivets were then forced through the holes when a man on the outside would use a pneumatic gun to form a rivet head. The rivet would then cool and contract. This technique caused the two sections of metal to be very tightly drawn together - which was as effective as a weld.

What with the extreme heat and noise (especially inside the boiler) this was a very distressing job.

ABOVE:
During the quiet winter months the company would make small pieces of machinery with a view to selling in the spring. This picture shows some cherry de-clusterers - these would remove the storks from the cherries.

Those were the days!

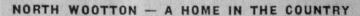